1 8 MAY 2018

Renewals

www.bromley.gov.uk/libraries

Bromley

THE LONDON BOROUGH
www.bromley.gov.uk

Please return/renew this item
by the last date shown.
Books may also be renewed by
phone and Internet.

The
FIRST OLYMPICS
of
✴Ancient Greece✴

by Lisa M. Bolt Simons

raintree 🏀
a Capstone company — publishers for children

Raintree is an imprint of Capstone Global Library Limited, a company incorporated in England and Wales having its registered office at 264 Banbury Road, Oxford, OX2, 7DY – Registered company number: 6695582

www.raintree.co.uk
myorders@raintree.co.uk

Edited by Aaron Sautter
Designed by Bobbie Nuytten
Picture research by Svetlana Zhurkin
Production by Jennifer Walker

ISBN 978 1 4747 1745 8
19 18 17 16 15
10 9 8 7 6 5 4 3 2 1

British Library Cataloguing in Publication Data
A full catalogue record for this book is available from the British Library.

Photo Credits

Alamy: Chronicle, 9, North Wind Picture Archives, 19, The Art Gallery Collection, 15 (top); Bridgeman Art Library: Look and Learn/Private Collection/Race of the Four Horse Chariots, Salinas, Alberto (1932-2004), 11; Corbis: National Geographic Society, 13; National Geographic Creative: H.M. Herget, 5; Newscom: akg-images, 6, EPA/Michael Kappeler, 20, Universal Images Group/Leemage, 17; Shutterstock: Attsetski (wreath), 21, Brian Maudsley, cover (front), 15 (bottom), Ensuper (paper), back cover and throughout, Henner Damke, 18, ilolab (grunge background), cover, 1, Kamira, back cover (bottom right), 10, Maxim Kostenko (background), 2 and throughout, mexrix, 7 (back), Netfalls Remy Musser, cover (back), 1, Roberto Castillo (column), back cover and throughout, Tatiana Popova, 8; XNR Productions, 7 (map)

We would like to thank Jonathan M. Hall, professor at the University of Chicago, for his invaluable help in the preparation of this book.

Printed and bound in China.

CONTENTS

LET THE GAMES BEGIN! 4

BEFORE THE GAMES 8

HORSE RACING EVENTS...............10

RUNNING EVENTS 12

ATHLETICS 14

BOXING AND WRESTLING 16

AWARD CEREMONIES 18

ANCIENT VS MODERN OLYMPICS 20

The athletes who became legends 21

Glossary 22

Read more...........................23

Websites 23

Comprehension questions....................24

Index 24

LET THE GAMES BEGIN!

Imagine you're in ancient Greece more than 2,700 years ago. Purple-robed judges, a trumpeter and a **herald** enter the arena. Several horse-drawn **chariots** soon follow. The crowd roars as athletes' names are announced. It's time for the Olympic games!

FACT:

Greek athletes usually competed while naked, to celebrate the human body and honour the gods.

4

Chariot races were a popular event in the ancient Olympics.

herald official at a competition who makes announcements to the crowd

chariot light, two-wheeled cart pulled by horses

5

The first Olympics took place in 776 BC. The games were held in Olympia. Only male Greek **citizens** could compete in the games. The Olympics lasted for five days every four years during a full summer moon. The moonlight allowed events and celebrations to continue into the night.

Olympia was home to several temples to the gods.

citizen member of a country or state who has the right to live there

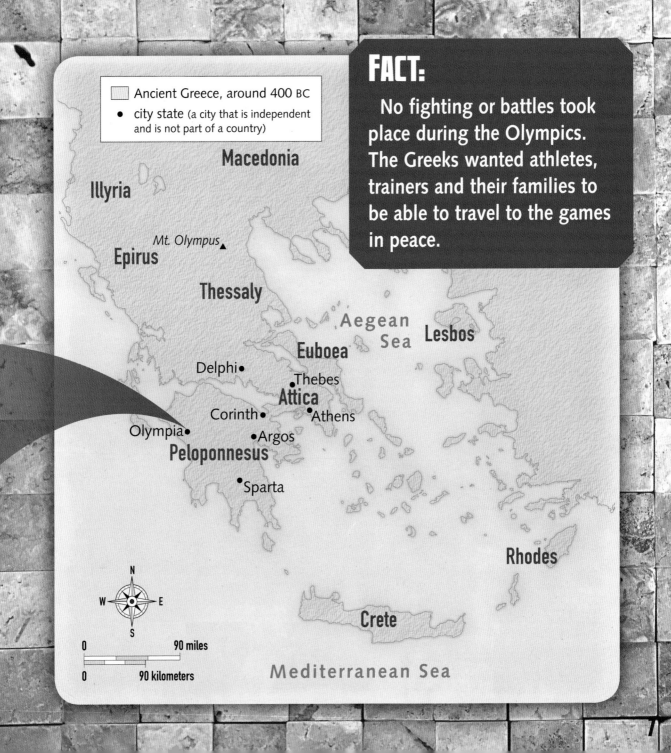

Ancient Greece, around 400 BC

● city state (a city that is independent and is not part of a country)

Macedonia

Illyria

Mt. Olympus ▲

Epirus

Thessaly

Aegean Sea

Lesbos

Euboea

Delphi ●

● Thebes

Attica

Corinth ●

● Athens

Olympia ●

● Argos

Peloponnesus

● Sparta

Rhodes

N
W ● E
S

0   90 miles

0   90 kilometers

Crete

Mediterranean Sea

7

BEFORE THE GAMES

Before the opening **ceremony**, athletes, trainers and judges took an **oath**. They promised to follow the rules and compete fairly. They also offered **sacrifices** of fruit and bronze items to the gods. Athletes prayed to the gods for victory.

ceremony special actions, words or music performed to mark an important event
oath serious, formal promise
sacrifice something offered as a gift to a god

bronze shield from ancient Greece

FACT:

On the third morning of the Olympics, another ceremony was held at the Temple of Zeus. Priests sacrificed 100 oxen to honour the king of the gods.

Athletes honoured Zeus at his temple in Olympia.

HORSE RACING EVENTS

Equestrian events had two kinds of races. Chariot races featured two- and four-horse chariots. Horses pulled the chariots around two poles in the **hippodrome** for 12 laps. These poles were about 400 metres (0.25 miles) apart. Normal horse races had six laps. The horse owners, not the riders, won the events.

ancient Greek vase with image of a chariot racer

equestrian to do with horses
hippodrome large, oval arena used for horse and chariot races

A Dangerous, Yet Thrilling Sport

Chariot racing was a dangerous sport. Chariot drivers often took risks. Sometimes they moved to the inside during tight turns. The move sometimes helped them get a lead. But it often resulted in crashes and serious injuries.

RUNNING EVENTS

The stadion was a 192-metre (630-foot) race. It was the first and only event of the original Olympics in 776 BC. Eventually, more races were added. These included races of 200 metres (656 feet), 400 metres (1,312 feet) and 4,800 metres (15,748 feet). Contestants ran barefoot on a track made of sand. Up to 20 athletes could run side by side.

FACT:

One Olympic race featured athletes wearing armour and a helmet. They ran 400 metres (1,312 feet) while carrying a shield.

ATHLETICS

The pentathlon was similar to modern athletics events. It included a race, long jump, wrestling, **discus** throw and **javelin** throw. The race was a sprint of almost 200 metres (656 ft). Athletes held weights in their hands for the long jump event. Wrestlers won by making an opponent fall three times. In discus and javelin events, athletes had five throws. The athlete with the longest throw won.

discus large, heavy disk that is thrown by an athlete

javelin light spear that is thrown by an athlete

discus throw competition in ancient Greece

THREE EVENTS OR FIVE?

Pentathlon contestants sometimes competed in only three events. If an athlete won the discus, javelin and long jump events, he was declared the pentathlon winner. If nobody won all three, athletes then competed in running and wrestling events.

BOXING AND WRESTLING

There were few rules in wrestling and boxing events. There was no ring and no time limit. A wrestler lost if he fell to his knees three times. Boxers won with a **knockout** or if an opponent raised his right hand to signal defeat. The pankration event was a mix of boxing, wrestling and **martial arts**.

knockout victory when a fighter's opponent is unable to get up after being knocked to the ground

martial arts styles of self-defence and fighting

During pankration matches, athletes could do almost anything to win. They could slap, punch and kick their opponents. An athlete won when his opponent gave up by tapping him on the shoulder or back.

AWARD CEREMONIES

Each event had two award ceremonies. Judges first gave palm branches to the event winners. Red ribbons were also tied to winners' heads and hands. On the last day of the games, the winners of all the events were announced. Olive tree wreaths were then placed on their heads.

Winning athletes were crowned with olive wreaths.

FACT:

Leonidas of Rhodes was the most successful athlete of the ancient Olympics. He won all his events in four straight Olympic games for a total of 12 olive wreaths.

ANCIENT VS MODERN OLYMPICS

Today's Olympics have changed from the ancient games. The modern games are held in different cities around the world. They take place every two years, alternating between the Summer and Winter Olympics. Ancient Greek athletes competed as individuals. Today's athletes compete in national teams from all over the world. The modern Olympics have changed over time, but the spirit of the ancient games lives on.

the 2012 Summer Olympics in London

The athletes who became legends

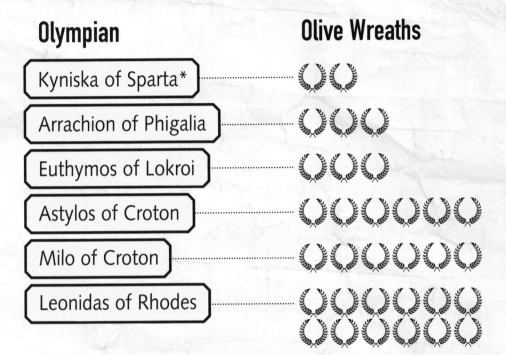

Olympian	Olive Wreaths
Kyniska of Sparta*	🏆🏆
Arrachion of Phigalia	🏆🏆🏆
Euthymos of Lokroi	🏆🏆🏆
Astylos of Croton	🏆🏆🏆🏆🏆🏆
Milo of Croton	🏆🏆🏆🏆🏆🏆
Leonidas of Rhodes	🏆🏆🏆🏆🏆🏆 🏆🏆🏆🏆🏆🏆

*the first woman to win; she was a horse owner

FACT:

In his last two Olympics, Astylos competed for Syracuse instead of his home city of Croton. This angered the people in Croton. They tore down the statue of Astylos and made his house into a prison.

Glossary

ceremony special actions, words or music performed to mark an important event

chariot light, two-wheeled cart pulled by horses

citizen member of a country or state who has the right to live there

discus large, heavy disk that is thrown by an athlete

equestrian to do with horses

herald official at a competition who makes announcements to the crowd

hippodrome large, oval arena used for horse and chariot races

javelin light spear that is thrown by an athlete

knockout victory when a fighter's opponent is unable to get up after being knocked to the ground

martial arts styles of self-defence and fighting

oath serious, formal promise

sacrifice something offered as a gift to a god

Read more

Ancient Greece (The History Detective Investigates), Rachel Minay (Wayland, 2015)

Ancient Greeks (History Showtime), Liza Phipps and Avril Thompson (Franklin Watts, 2015)

The World of Olympics (The Olympics), Nick Hunter (Raintree, 2012)

Websites

www.bbc.co.uk/history/anicent/greeks/
Explore topics about the ancient Greeks, such as the Olympic Games, theatres and gods.

www.olympic.org
Visit the official Olympic Games website for photos and information on future games.